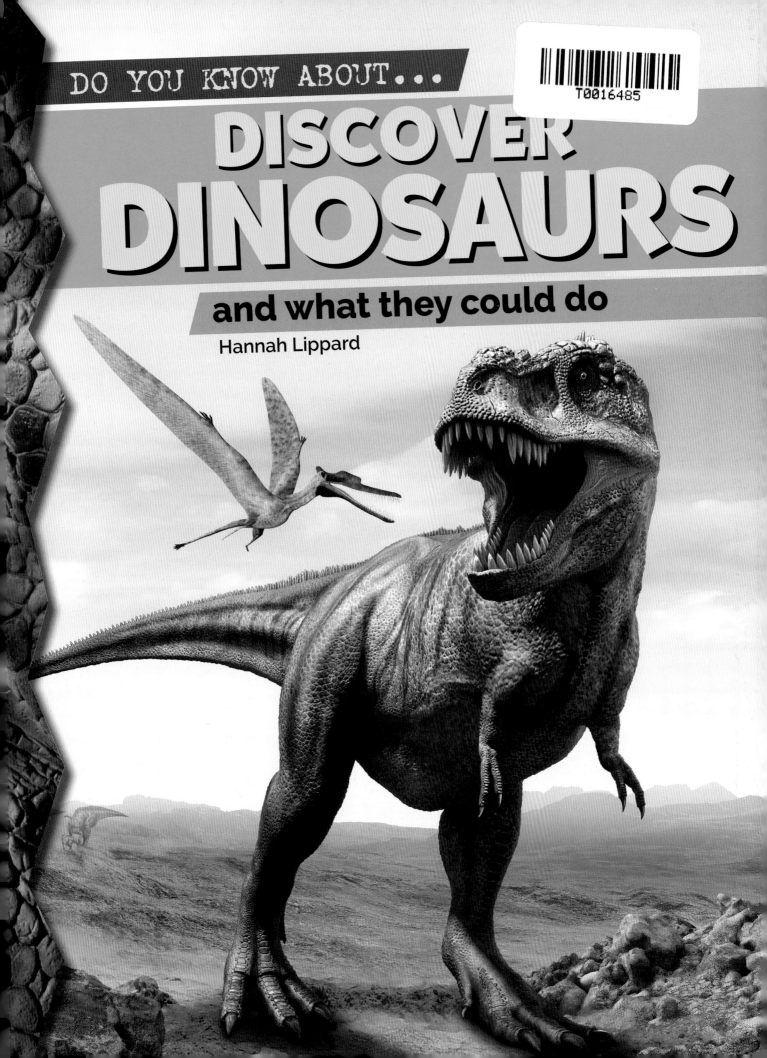

DO YOU KNOW ABOUT...

DISCOVER DINOSAURS

and what they could do

Hannah Lippard

www.FlowerpotPress.com
CHC-0912-0477
ISBN: 978-1-4867-2107-8
Made in China/Fabriqué en Chine

Table of Contents

DO YOU KNOW ABOUT...

How much do you know about dinosaurs? Find awesome facts throughout the book as you learn more about these prehistoric creatures that existed long ago. Just look for Do You Know About... facts throughout the book!

The Mesozoic Era

The Mesozoic era was a geologic era from 251.9 to 66 million years ago. The word Mesozoic means "middle animals." During the Mesozoic era, the types of animals and plants living on Earth changed significantly. The era is best known for being the time when dinosaurs lived. Dinosaurs evolved early in the Mesozoic era and became extinct at the end of it.

Triassic Period

The Triassic period was the first period of the Mesozoic era. It lasted from 251.9 to 201.3 million years ago. At the beginning of the Triassic, the continents of the world were connected in one huge supercontinent called Pangaea. Later, Pangaea started to separate into two continents. This separation continued into the Jurassic period. Dinosaurs first appeared during the Triassic period. They evolved from a group of reptiles called archosaurs.

LAURASIA

TETHYS SEA

Equator

GONDWANA

Plateosaurus

DO YOU KNOW ABOUT...

Geologic History

Geology is the science of the history of Earth and the life on it, or geologic history. Geologic history is divided into different units of time. Eras are one of these units. The dinosaurs lived during the Mesozoic era, and the current era is called the Cenozoic era. Eras are subdivided into smaller units of time called geologic periods. The three periods of the Mesozoic era are the Triassic, Jurassic, and Cretaceous periods.

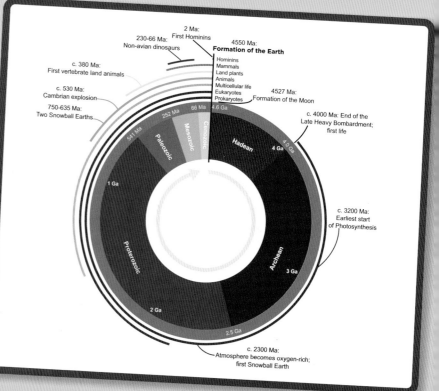

2 Ma: First Hominins

230-66 Ma: Non-avian dinosaurs

4550 Ma: Formation of the Earth

Hominins
Mammals
Land plants
Animals
Multicellular life
Eukaryotes
Prokaryotes

c. 380 Ma: First vertebrate land animals

c. 530 Ma: Cambrian explosion

4527 Ma: Formation of the Moon

750-635 Ma: Two Snowball Earths

252 Ma   66 Ma   4.6 Ga

c. 4000 Ma: End of the Late Heavy Bombardment; first life

541 Ma

Paleozoic   Mesozoic   Cenozoic

Hadean   4.0 Ga   4 Ga

1 Ga

c. 3200 Ma: Earliest start of Photosynthesis

Proterozoic   Archean   3 Ga

2 Ga

2.5 Ga

c. 2300 Ma: Atmosphere becomes oxygen-rich; first Snowball Earth

Cryolophosaurus

Jurassic Period

The Jurassic period was the second period of the Mesozoic era. It lasted from 201.3 to 145 million years ago. Because of the separation of Pangaea and warmer temperatures around the world, dinosaurs became the dominant animals. Dinosaurs also diversified, which means they evolved into a variety of different kinds.

DO YOU KNOW ABOUT...

Mass Extinctions

The Mesozoic era began and ended with mass extinctions, also called extinction events. In a mass extinction, many species become extinct during a relatively short period of time. The Permian-Triassic extinction event occurred at the end of the Permian period (the last period before the Mesozoic era). It was the largest mass extinction ever, and about 90 percent of all species on the planet died. The Cretaceous-Paleogene extinction event occurred at the end of the Cretaceous period (the last period of the Mesozoic era). Over half of species went extinct, including all remaining dinosaurs. The cause may have been an asteroid striking Earth, volcanic activity, or both.

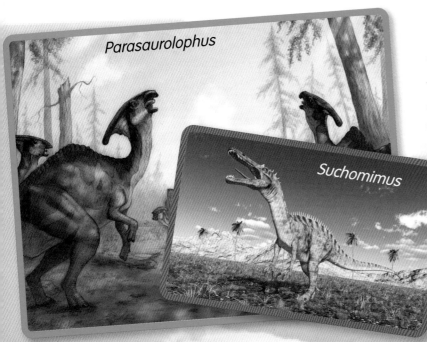
Parasaurolophus

Suchomimus

Cretaceous Period

The Cretaceous period was the third period of the Mesozoic era. It lasted from 145 to 66 million years ago, making it the longest period of the era. The continents continued to drift apart during the Cretaceous period, and by the end of it they were much closer to their current positions. Some dinosaur species went extinct, and others lived until the extinction event at the end of the Cretaceous period. The only dinosaurs to survive past the Cretaceous period were birds.

Dinosaur Taxonomy

Taxonomy is the classification of plants and animals based on characteristics they have in common with each other. All dinosaurs were members of Dinosauria, a group called a clade. They were terrestrial reptiles. They had strong back legs that moved underneath their bodies, instead of on the side like lizards. Their legs could support a large body size and allowed them to stand upright and to run. Their skulls were strong and lightweight. But despite all these similarities, dinosaurs are a very diverse clade with many differences.

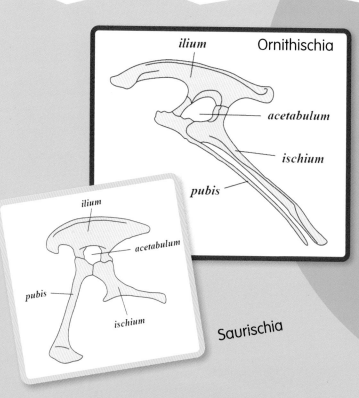

ilium
Ornithischia
acetabulum
ischium
pubis

ilium
acetabulum
pubis
ischium

Saurischia

Ornithischia and Saurischia

Ornithischia (meaning "bird-hipped") and Saurischia (meaning "lizard-hipped") are the two main groups dinosaurs are usually split into. In taxonomy, they are called orders. The main difference between these groups is the dinosaurs' hip bones. In Ornithischian dinosaurs, a bone called the pubis points to the back. In Saurischian dinosaurs, the pubis points to the front. Ornithischians are almost all herbivores. Saurischians may be herbivores or carnivores. Ornithischians did not appear until the Jurassic period, but Saurischians first lived in the Triassic period.

DO YOU KNOW ABOUT...

Taxons

Groups of similar organisms are called taxons, and they occur in ranks from the largest type of group (domain) to the smallest (species). Animals sharing the same species are much more closely related than those only sharing the same domain. The dinosaurs you will read about in this book are classified by genus, which is one rank higher than species. Paleontologists have discovered over 500 different genera of dinosaurs, and there might be more than 1,300 yet to be discovered.

SPECIES
GENUS
FAMILY
ORDER
CLASS
PHYLUM
KINGDOM
DOMAIN

Theropoda and Sauropodomorpha

Theropoda and Sauropodomorpha are two subgroups—called suborders—of Saurischia. Theropods were carnivores. They usually walked on their two back legs and had short front legs. Sauropodomorphs were herbivores. They usually walked on all four legs and had long necks and tails. Sauropodomorphs were often larger than theropods.

Theropod

Sauropodomorph

DO YOU KNOW ABOUT...

New Developments

Dinosaurs have been extinct for millions of years, but we are still learning new things about them. Recently, some scientists suggested that the Saurischian and Ornithischian categories should be changed. They think theropods are more closely related to Ornithischians than to sauropodomorphs. The new groups would be called Saurischians and Ornithoscelidans.

Non-Dinosaurs

Not all large Mesozoic animals were dinosaurs. Sometimes people mistake pterosaurs and plesiosaurs for dinosaurs. However, pterosaurs were flying reptiles that belonged to the clade Pterosauria, not Dinosauria. Plesiosaurs were swimming reptiles that belonged to the clade Plesiosauria, not Dinosauria. Sometimes even woolly mammoths are called dinosaurs, but they are mammals, not reptiles. Woolly mammoths did not live in the Mesozoic era at all. They lived millions of years after the end of the Cretaceous period and interacted with humans.

Pterosaur

Woolly Mammoth

Plesiosaur

Eoraptor

Eoraptor (ee-oh-RAP-ter) was a dinosaur that still poses many questions for paleontologists. As one of the first dinosaurs to ever exist, it was like a template for later dinosaurs to evolve from. It lived at the same time as the ancestors of dinosaurs, long before dinosaurs became the dominant animal. *Eoraptor* had features of different types of later dinosaurs.

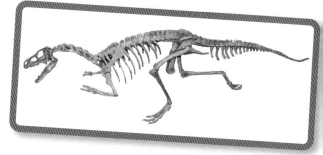

Dino Fast Facts

Name meaning: "dawn plunderer"
Type: Saurischian (unknown)
Period: late Triassic
Location: Argentina
Diet: omnivore

The First Dinosaur?

Eoraptor may be the earliest known dinosaur! It was first discovered in 1991 in a fossil site in Argentina called the Valley of the Moon. Scientists were not sure whether the skeleton was from a juvenile or adult dinosaur. It had large eye sockets and skull bones that were not entirely connected, which means it may have still been growing when it died.

Valley of the Moon

DO YOU KNOW ABOUT...

Eoraptor's Competition

A recent discovery could replace *Eoraptor* as the earliest dinosaur. *Nyasasaurus* was discovered in Tanzania and is thought to be around 243 million years old. Paleontologists are not sure whether *Nyasasaurus* is an actual dinosaur or just a relative of early dinosaurs.

Nyasasaurus

Small but Speedy

Eoraptor was a very small dinosaur. It was about 3 feet (.9 meters) long and it weighed up to about 25 pounds (11.3 kilograms). Although *Eoraptor* was little, it had long legs that made it a fast runner. This was important, because *Eoraptor* had to compete for food with the archosaurs, ancestors of dinosaurs that still existed in the Triassic period. It also had to escape from predators, possibly including other early dinosaurs like *Herrerasaurus*.

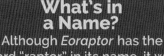

DO YOU KNOW ABOUT...

What's in a Name?

Although *Eoraptor* has the word "raptor" in its name, it was not actually a raptor. Raptors were predatory dinosaurs that lived during the Cretaceous period. Unlike *Eoraptor*, they had long curved claws on their back feet. Other "raptors" that aren't actually raptors include *Gigantoraptor*, *Oviraptor*, and *Megaraptor*. To make the situation more confusing, some true raptors do not have "raptor" in their names!

Gigantoraptor

Theropod or Sauropodomorph?

Paleontologists are still unsure whether *Eoraptor* was an early theropod or an early sauropodomorph— or neither. Some think *Eoraptor* was such an early Saurischian that the theropods and sauropodomorphs had not split apart yet. *Eoraptor* had two different tooth shapes, so it was probably an omnivore. Its front teeth were long, sharp, and curved back for eating meat like a theropod. Its back teeth were blunt and leaf-shaped for eating plants like a sauropodomorph. Originally, *Eoraptor* was classified as a theropod. But the discovery of *Eodromaeus*, another early dinosaur, suggests that *Eoraptor* may be a sauropodomorph. *Eodromaeus* has only sharp teeth, as well as other features shared with later theropods. Since it lived at the same time as *Eoraptor* but *Eoraptor* lacked these features, *Eoraptor* might not be a theropod after all.

Eodromaeus

Eoraptor

Herrerasaurus

Like *Eoraptor*, *Herrerasaurus* (huh-reh-ruh-SAWR-us) was one of the earliest dinosaurs. It was about 12 feet (3.7 meters) long. Unlike *Eoraptor*, *Herrerasaurus* only ate meat. It was good at hunting, but it was also prey for Triassic archosaurs that were larger than *Herrerasaurus*. The dinosaur was named after Victorino Herrera, a farmer who discovered the first *Herrerasaurus* skeleton.

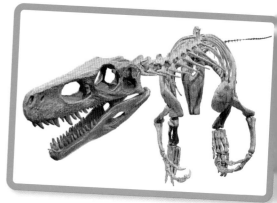

Dino Fast Facts

Name meaning: "Herrera's lizard"
Type: Saurischian (theropod)
Period: late Triassic
Location: Argentina
Diet: carnivore

Herrerasaurus the Hunter

Herrerasaurus may have eaten other dinosaurs, archosaurs, and therapsids (small animals that were the ancestors of mammals). *Herrerasaurus* had multiple adaptations to make it an effective predator. Its hands had three claws that curved backward and could grab or injure prey. Its lower jaw was flexible and had sharp teeth that curved back for holding prey. Its back legs were strong and tall for running quickly on two feet. It lived in humid, cool areas with trees and ferns that kept it hidden from the animals it hunted.

Out of the Box

Because *Herrerasaurus* was such an early dinosaur, it had characteristics of both non-dinosaur archosaurs and later, more evolved dinosaurs. For example, its leg and wrist bones resembled archosaurs, but its pelvic bones and backbones resembled Jurassic and Cretaceous dinosaurs. This made *Herrerasaurus* difficult to classify. Many paleontologists today consider *Herrerasaurus* a basal theropod, meaning it was one of the earliest and most primitive theropods. But like *Eoraptor*, some scientists question whether *Herrerasaurus* was a true dinosaur or an evolved archosaur ancestor.

DO YOU KNOW ABOUT...

The Evolution of Wings

The forelimbs of *Herrerasaurus* look strange when compared to other Triassic reptiles'. However, they were somewhat similar to modern bird wings. They might have been able to fold up like the wings of a pigeon, and they might have had feathers. Some paleontologists think *Herrerasaurus* marked a step in the evolution of wings and flight that led the way to birds!

Dinosaur Origins

South American Origins

All *Herrerasaurus* fossils have been found in the Valley of the Moon in Argentina, the same place *Eoraptor* was first found. Paleontologists think that dinosaurs first appeared in South America before spreading to the rest of the world, so it makes sense *Herrerasaurus* and *Eoraptor* were both found there.

Plateosaurus

Plateosaurus (pla-tee-uh-SAWR-us) was not only one of the first dinosaurs to exist, it was also one of the first dinosaurs to be discovered by humans when it was found in 1834. It probably moved on just two feet, because the palms on its forelimbs faced each other and could not be used to walk on the ground. In 1997, a *Plateosaurus* bone was the first dinosaur fossil found in Norway, proving that dinosaurs once lived there.

Dino Fast Facts

Name meaning: "flat lizard"
Type: Saurischian (sauropodomorph)
Period: late Triassic
Location: France, Germany, Switzerland, and Norway
Diet: herbivore

Swallowing Rocks

Plateosaurus was herbivorous and ate food like the leaves from coniferous trees and ferns. It could reach higher than smaller plant-eating dinosaurs because of its long neck. *Plateosaurus* had sharp teeth to cut the leaves off their plants, but it did not have teeth that could grind the leaves to make them digestible. It may have used gastroliths to grind the plants instead. Gastroliths are stones that an animal swallows. Once they are in the animal's stomach, they grind up food to help the animal digest it.

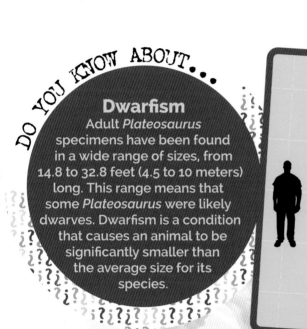

Thumb Claw

Plateosaurus hands had five fingers. Their thumbs were large and partially opposable, which made it easier for them to take hold of leaves and branches. Their thumbs also had large claws on them. These claws may have been used for digging, fighting, or cutting plants for food. *Plateosaurus'* thumb claw is probably also related to its ability to stand on two legs. That way the dinosaur could reach higher plant material and use its thumbs to help grab it.

DO YOU KNOW ABOUT...

Dwarfism

Adult *Plateosaurus* specimens have been found in a wide range of sizes, from 14.8 to 32.8 feet (4.5 to 10 meters) long. This range means that some *Plateosaurus* were likely dwarves. Dwarfism is a condition that causes an animal to be significantly smaller than the average size for its species.

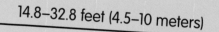

14.8–32.8 feet (4.5–10 meters)

Prosauropods

Plateosaurus is sometimes called a prosauropod. The prosauropods were a group of Triassic and early Jurassic sauropodomorphs. They are the ancestors of the sauropods, the sauropodomorphs of the Jurassic and Cretaceous periods. Both prosauropods and sauropods had long necks and tails, small heads, and big bodies. But prosauropods were much smaller than sauropods. Prosauropods could be bipedal (walking on two feet), quadrupedal (walking on four feet), or a combination of both, but sauropods were always quadrupeds.

Melanorosaurus

Melanorosaurus (meh-luh-nor-uh-SAWR-us) was named after the mountain where the first two specimens were found. Most early dinosaurs were small, carnivorous bipeds, but *Melanorosaurus* was a large dinosaur that ate plants and walked on four legs.

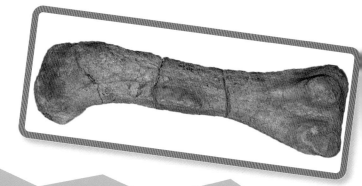

Dino Fast Facts

Name meaning: "Black Mountain lizard"
Type: Saurischian (sauropodomorph)
Period: late Triassic
Location: South Africa
Diet: herbivore or omnivore

Big and Strong

Melanorosaurus was one of the largest animals of its time. It was about 26 feet (7.9 meters) long and weighed around 2,500 pounds (1,134 kilograms). That is eight times longer and 100 times heavier than *Eoraptor,* which was possibly a fellow early sauropodomorph. To support its weight, *Melanorosaurus* had strong wide legs. It also had a long tail and neck, which helped it stay balanced.

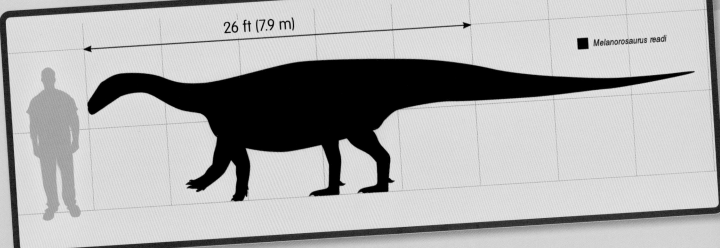

26 ft (7.9 m)

■ *Melanorosaurus readi*

Melanorosaurus on the Move

Melanorosaurus may have traveled in groups called flocks. This might have been for protection from predators, or it might have been for socialization with other dinosaurs of the same species. *Melanorosaurus* walked slowly, both during the day and during the night. In the afternoon, it rested under tall trees to avoid the heat. *Melanorosaurus* also probably used trees for food. Its long neck let it reach the leaves at the tops of trees.

DO YOU KNOW ABOUT...

Family in Argentina

The closest relative to *Melanorosaurus* was a dinosaur called *Riojasaurus*. *Riojasaurus* lived in Argentina like *Eoraptor* and *Herrerasaurus*. That means two closely related dinosaurs were from two different continents: *Melanorosaurus* from Africa and *Riojasaurus* from South America. This is possible because those continents had not entirely separated from each other yet. During the Triassic period, they were part of the southern continent called Gondwana.

Riojasaurus

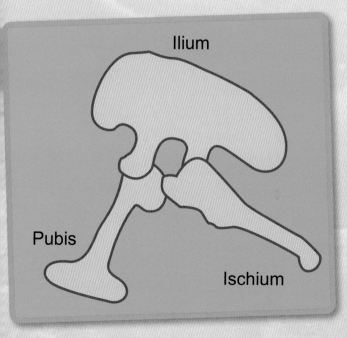

Ilium

Pubis

Ischium

Keep Your Feet on the Ground

Paleontologists think *Melanorosaurus* walked on four legs, which is normal for large dinosaurs of its shape. However, they may have had bipedal abilities as well. *Melanorosaurus* had shorter front legs and longer pubic bones than its relative *Riojasaurus*. This makes sense if *Melanorosaurus* spent some time standing on only its back legs. The shorter front legs would not need to carry as much weight, and the longer pubic bones would help support the dinosaur's stomach. This means *Melanorosaurus* was a facultative biped. In other words, it stood on two legs some of the time and on four at other times, depending on its situation and needs.

Coelophysis

Coelophysis (see-luh-FIE-sis) might have been the first dinosaur to live in North America. It was a typical early dinosaur: small, up to 9 feet (2.7 meters) long, and carnivorous. It was descended from the very first basal dinosaurs. *Coelophysis* was first discovered in 1881, but it was not very well understood. Then in 1947, many more *Coelophysis* skeletons were found in New Mexico. Some of the skeletons were not missing any bones, making them the oldest complete skeletons to ever be discovered. The quarry the specimens came from may contain 1,000 near complete fossils.

Dino Fast Facts

Name meaning: "hollow form"
Type: Saurischian (theropod)
Period: late Triassic
Location: South Africa, United States, and Zimbabwe
Diet: carnivore

Hollow Bones and Wishbones

Coelophysis was named for its hollow bones. They made the dinosaur light so it could move quickly and gracefully, which was important for avoiding predators and finding prey. *Coelophysis* was also one of the very first dinosaurs to have a wishbone. A wishbone, also called a furcula, is a forked bone found in modern birds. *Coelophysis* and birds are related, but not closely, because birds only evolved from dinosaurs beginning in the Jurassic period.

Not fused

Coelophysis	Allosaurus	Velociraptor	Archeopteryx	Columba
Theropods			Birds	

DO YOU KNOW ABOUT...

State Fossil

The *Coelophysis* bones discovered in Ghost Ranch, New Mexico, were from dinosaurs of all different ages: hatchlings, juveniles, teenagers, and adults. Before this discovery, there were not many *Coelophysis* fossils at all. It was such an important find that New Mexico made *Coelophysis* its official state fossil.

Predation Techniques

Coelophysis had very big eyes. This adaptation helped it find prey, similar to a modern-day hawk. Because of its large eyes, the dinosaur had a large brain, too, which it used to understand what it saw. *Coelophysis* may have hunted in large groups. Since so many skeletons were found together, paleontologists think they might have been a herd animal like *Melanorosaurus*. Today, herd behavior is more common for prey than predators, as moving in groups is safer.

DO YOU KNOW ABOUT...

Cannibalism Accusations

Some *Coelophysis* specimens have been found with the remains of small reptiles inside their stomachs. Scientists used to think this might mean that the dinosaurs ate their own offspring. Later they realized that the reptiles were not other dinosaurs at all—they were small archosaurs. Dinosaurs evolved from early archosaurs, but that does not mean these archosaurs immediately went extinct when the dinosaurs appeared. The times of archosaurs and dinosaurs overlapped by about 20 million years.

Coelophysis bauri

20 in (50.8 cm)

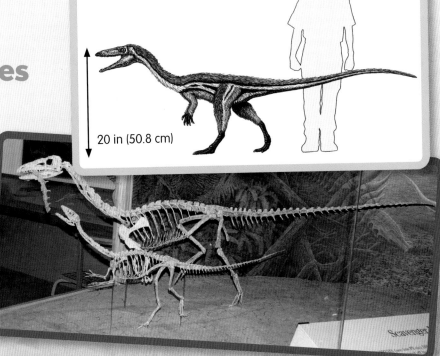

Different Body Types

Not all *Coelophysis* looked the same. They had two different body plans. One was smaller, about 33 pounds (15 kilograms), and is called "gracile." The other was larger, about 44 pounds (20 kilograms), and is called "robust." The differences might have been related to gender. However, paleontologists do not know which body plan was female and which was male.

Heterodontosaurus

Heterodontosaurus (heh-tuh-ro-don-tuh-SAWR-us) was a very small dinosaur. It was about 3 to 5 feet (0.9 to 1.5 meters) long. It is best known for its unusual teeth, which inspired its name. It was one of the earliest Ornithischians.

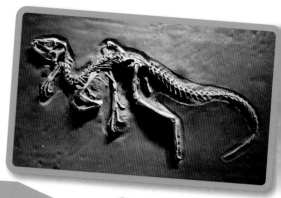

Dino Fast Facts

Name meaning: "different-toothed lizard"
Type: Ornithischian
Period: early Jurassic
Location: South Africa and Lesotho
Diet: unknown

A

B

The Different-Toothed Lizard

Most dinosaurs had mouths full of just one type of teeth. This is common in reptiles. *Heterodontosaurus*, on the other hand, had three different types of teeth. The incisor teeth (located in the front) were sharp and used for cutting. The molar teeth (located in the back) were flat and used for grinding. The canine teeth (located between the incisors and molars) were cone-shaped and enlarged to form two tusks.

What Did Heterodontosaurus Use Its Tusks For?

Paleontologists used to think that *Heterodontosaurus'* tusks were used in competition for mates. Then they discovered that juvenile *Heterodontosaurus* also had tusks, not just the adults. If the tusks were used for mating, young dinosaurs would not need to grow them yet. So paleontologists theorized that the tusks were used for catching small prey like lizards, insects, or therapsids. It is also possible that *Heterodontosaurus* used them for cutting into the skins or shells of plants, or even for digging in the dirt.

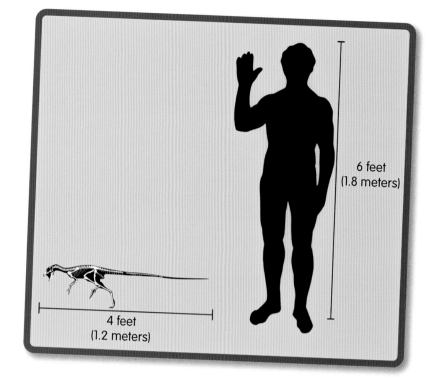

6 feet
(1.8 meters)

4 feet
(1.2 meters)

DO YOU KNOW ABOUT...

Omnivorous and Ornithischian

The idea that *Heterodontosaurus* ate meat is surprising. *Heterodontosaurus* was an Ornithischian, and Ornithischians were usually herbivores. How is it possible for an Ornithischian to be omnivorous? Ornithischians shared a common ancestor with Saurischians. It was probably a small carnivore, like most early dinosaurs. So Ornithischians had to evolve from eating meat to eating plants. Since *Heterodontosaurus* is one of the earliest Ornithischians, it might have been in the middle of that transition.

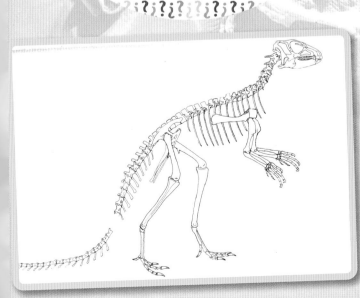

Opposable Fingers

Heterodontosaurus had five-fingered hands. The fourth and fifth fingers on each hand might have been opposable, which was rare for dinosaurs, especially meat-eating dinosaurs. This would make it possible for *Heterodontosaurus* to pick up objects with one hand instead of two. *Heterodontosaurus* probably used this special ability to grasp plants or catch small prey. This made it more skilled and graceful with its hands than most other dinosaurs.

Allosaurus

Allosaurus (a-luh-SAWR-us) was a large and powerful carnivorous dinosaur, probably the most formidable predator during the late Jurassic period. It was one of the first dinosaurs to be discovered by paleontologists, and many specimens have been found. This means scientists know more about *Allosaurus* than many other dinosaurs. Most *Allosaurus* fossils were found in Utah, where *Allosaurus* was the most common carnivore. Today, *Allosaurus* is Utah's state fossil.

Dino Fast Facts

Name meaning: "other lizard"
Type: Saurischian (theropod)
Period: late Jurassic
Location: United States and Portugal
Diet: carnivore

Take a Bite

A dinosaur's gape is how wide it can open its mouth. *Allosaurus* had a huge gape of 79 degrees! This was possible because its skull was wider in the back than in the front, so its jaws were large and strong. *Allosaurus* might have used its wide gape to attack dinosaurs larger than itself or to slash with its teeth instead of bite. *Allosaurus* had deadly teeth: 2 to 4 inches (5.1 to 10.2 centimeters) long, curved backward to keep prey from escaping, and serrated (notched on the edges) for cutting.

DO YOU KNOW ABOUT...

Big Al

Allosaurus was usually 25 to 35 feet (7.6 to 10.7 meters) long, but some may have measured 40 feet (12.2 meters)! One specimen, nicknamed Big Al, is estimated to have weighed over 3,300 pounds (1,496.9 kilograms) when it was alive. Despite this impressive size, *Allosaurus* was still smaller than many sauropods and than four other predatory dinosaurs, including *Tyrannosaurus*.

40 feet (12.2 meters)

6 feet (1.8 meters)

Hunting and Scavenging

Allosaurus mostly ate herbivorous dinosaurs. Fossil evidence suggests that it attacked *Stegosaurus* regularly. Paleontologists have found an *Allosaurus* tail bone and pelvic bone with injuries shaped like a *Stegosaurus* tail spike, and a *Stegosaurus* neck bone with an injury shaped like *Allosaurus'* jaws. If *Allosaurus* hunted by itself, it could probably only attack medium-sized herbivores. If it hunted in packs, it may have been able to attack large herbivores like *Apatosaurus*. In addition to hunting, *Allosaurus* probably scavenged, which means it ate animals that were already dead when it found them.

DO YOU KNOW ABOUT...

Optimal Tension

A big bite does not necessarily mean a better bite. The ideal gape for *Allosaurus*, called optimal tension, was about 30 degrees. *Allosaurus* may have used different techniques—both a wide slash and a smaller bite—to be a more flexible, adaptable, and successful predator.

A Natural Crown

The smallest bones in *Allosaurus'* skull, called lacrimal bones, extended out of its body over its eyes. They formed two small horns. *Allosaurus* also had two ridges connected to the horns that ran along the top of its nose bones. The horns and the ridge together formed a crest, a feature found on the heads of some dinosaurs (including birds). *Allosaurus* may have used its crest to attract mates or recognize other dinosaurs.

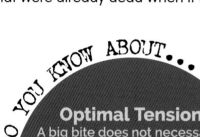

Stegosaurus

Stegosaurus (steh-guh-SAWR-us) walked slowly and lived on a diet of plants. When confronted with predators like *Allosaurus*, it relied on its spiky tail for protection. But *Stegosaurus* is best known for the plates on its back, whose purpose is still unknown.

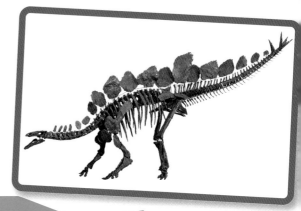

Dino Fast Facts

Name meaning: "roofed lizard"
Type: Ornithischian
Period: late Jurassic
Location: United States and Portugal
Diet: herbivore

Built-In Armor

The triangular plates on *Stegosaurus'* back were connected to the dinosaur by its skin, not its skeleton, and they were made of bone. They might have scared away potential predators. They might have been for display, like attracting mates or recognizing other *Stegosaurus* dinosaurs, similar to the horns and ridge of *Allosaurus*. Or they might have controlled *Stegosaurus'* body temperature using blood vessels to release or collect heat. This process is called thermoregulation.

DO YOU KNOW ABOUT...
Plates Mistake

When *Stegosaurus* skeletons fossilized, the plates usually separated from the rest of the bones. A paleontologist studying the first *Stegosaurus* specimen thought that the plates had been in a flat position on its back. Later, a specimen was found with the plates held in place by mud, proving that they stood straight up to the sides of the dinosaur's spine.

Tail or Weapon?

Stegosaurus had a flexible tail with two pairs of long spikes on the end. They were made out of bone covered in keratin (the substance that horns are made of). Cartoonist Gary Larson was the first to jokingly refer to the tail spikes as a "thagomizer" in one of his comics, which scientists then adopted themselves. *Stegosaurus* probably used its thagomizers to defend against predators like *Allosaurus*. About 10 percent of the spikes discovered by paleontologists were damaged, as if they had been used in a fight. *Stegosaurus* could have weaponized its thagomizers in two ways. If it was standing parallel to a predator, it could cut or slash with the spikes. If it was standing at a different angle, the spikes would have stuck in the predator and broken off from *Stegosaurus*. This would have hurt both of the dinosaurs.

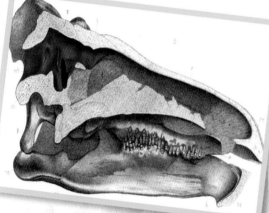

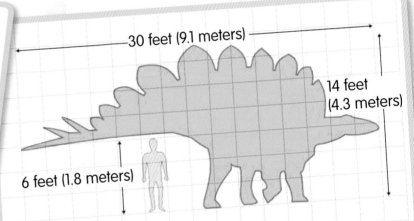

30 feet (9.1 meters)

14 feet (4.3 meters)

6 feet (1.8 meters)

Big Animal, Small Brain

Stegosaurus' skull and brain were very small in proportion to its body size. *Stegosaurus* was about the size of a small bus, but its brain was only the size of a hot dog! Paleontologists used to think that, in addition to its small brain, *Stegosaurus* had a bundle of nerves to manage its movement. They called this an auxiliary brain. These nerves would have been located in the dinosaur's spinal cord above its back legs. But now paleontologists think the space in the spinal cord was likely used for storing energy. This is similar to modern birds.

Diplodocus

Diplodocus (duh-PLAH-duh-kus) is one of the longest known dinosaurs! It was 85 feet (25.9 meters) long on average, but it could have grown to about 100 feet (30.5 meters). This impressive length is mostly due to *Diplodocus*' long neck, which was about 26 feet (7.9 meters) and tail, which was about 45 feet (13.7 meters). *Diplodocus* weighed about 12 to 15 tons (10.9 to 13.6 metric tons), which sounds like a huge amount, but was very light for the dinosaur's size.

Dino Fast Facts

Name meaning: "double beam"
Type: Saurischian (sauropodomorph)
Period: late Jurassic
Location: United States
Diet: herbivore

Balancing Act

Diplodocus' tail was probably a counterbalance for its neck. That means that the weight of its tail and neck balanced each other to keep the dinosaur steady. Both the neck and tail contained vertebrae, the bones that make up the spinal column. But *Diplodocus*' neck had 15 very long vertebrae, and its tail had 80 short vertebrae. This meant its tail was more flexible than its neck. *Diplodocus* may have been able to whip its tail at 800 miles (1,287.5 kilometers) per hour, faster than the speed of sound. This would have made a loud cracking noise.

DO YOU KNOW ABOUT...

How Diplodocus Used Its Whip Tail

If *Diplodocus* used its tail like a weapon and struck another dinosaur, it probably would have broken some of its tail bones in the process. It would have been safer to use the tail as an intimidation tactic. The sound might have been as loud as the boom of a cannon, scaring potential predators away.

How Did Diplodocus Eat?

Most of the time, *Diplodocus* probably held its neck in a horizontal position or lifted at about a 45-degree angle. Paleontologists are not sure whether *Diplodocus'* neck was flexible enough to reach the ground or the treetops without moving its body. Either way, it could have reached up high by standing on its two back legs. Then it used the small teeth in the front of its mouth to strip leaves from the trees. *Diplodocus* was also able to eat low-down plants like ferns, because its front legs were shorter than its back legs, making the front of its body closer to the ground. *Diplodocus* did not have teeth in the back of its mouth for chewing. Instead, food stayed in its stomach for a long time as it was broken down and digested.

DO YOU KNOW ABOUT...

Tooth Replacement

Diplodocus had delicate teeth, but it had to eat a lot of tree leaves and ferns. This damaged the teeth over time. As a result, *Diplodocus* lost its teeth more often than many other dinosaurs. Luckily, it could replace its lost teeth, at an impressive rate of almost 1 tooth per month!

How Did Diplodocus Walk?

Because of its long tail, *Diplodocus'* center of mass (the place where its mass was concentrated) was far back in its body. This meant *Diplodocus* had to walk very slowly. About a century ago, paleontologists thought that its legs were splayed out to the side, like a lizard's legs. This was a problem, because *Diplodocus'* stomach was so large it would have needed a ditch or a hole underneath it to keep from dragging on the ground! Later, paleontologists found *Diplodocus* footprints that showed it walked with its legs straight underneath it.

Brachiosaurus

Brachiosaurus (brah-kee-oh-SAWR-us), like *Diplodocus*, was a sauropod, so it was quadrupedal and herbivorous. It was also found in the same area as *Diplodocus*, the western United States. Unlike *Diplodocus*, *Brachiosaurus* had longer front legs than back legs, was very heavy at up to 60 tons (54.4 metric tons) or more, and had a tail much shorter than its neck. In fact, it may not have looked anything like the other dinosaurs in the area where it lived!

Dino Fast Facts

Name meaning: "arm lizard"
Type: Saurischian (sauropodomorph)
Period: late Jurassic
Location: United States
Diet: herbivore

The Giraffe Dinosaur

Most sauropods had longer back legs than front legs, like *Diplodocus*. *Brachiosaurus* was named the "arm lizard" because its front legs were longer than its back legs. This made its back slope and its neck naturally point higher, like a giraffe. *Brachiosaurus'* long forelimbs were an adaptation that allowed the dinosaur to reach food in tall trees without hurting its neck. The adaptation was especially helpful since *Brachiosaurus'* center of mass was too far forward for it to stand on two feet for very long.

85 feet (25.9 meters)

DO YOU KNOW ABOUT...

Walking on Tiptoes

All dinosaurs, including *Brachiosaurus*, walked with their heels never touching the ground. This means they were digitigrade animals, or animals that walk on their toes. The opposite of a digitigrade is a plantigrade, an animal that walks on the soles of its feet with its heels touching the ground. Humans are plantigrades. Digitigrade animals have longer feet, because their ankle bones are higher on their legs. Other digitigrades include cats, birds, and dogs.

No Climbing or Swimming Allowed

Brachiosaurus probably avoided hills, because its large size made walking on a steep surface dangerous. It also probably stayed out of the water, because it might have slipped on the muddy floor, and because it might have had air pockets in its body that could have made it float and move very unsteadily. Despite these challenges, paleontologists used to think that *Brachiosaurus* was an aquatic dinosaur! This is because it had such a long neck and a bump high on its head. The researchers thought its nostrils were located on the bump to be used like a snorkel.

Browsing Habits

Brachiosaurus was so large that, like other sauropods, it needed to eat about 240 pounds (108.9 kilograms) of plants every single day. Paleontologists are not certain whether *Brachiosaurus* was a high browser or a low browser, but it likely favored high-growing plants while occasionally eating low-growing plants. Its main sources of food were probably coniferous trees, ginkgo trees, and plants called cycads that resemble ferns. *Brachiosaurus* probably lived in flocks. Once a flock had eaten all the vegetation available in an area, it would travel to a new place to live.

Iguanodon

Iguanodon (ih-GWAH-nuh-don) was the second dinosaur ever to be named. It was named nearly 200 years ago, in 1825. Then in 1842, the group Dinosauria was created, and *Iguanodon* was one of only three dinosaurs included. Since then, paleontologists have continued to research *Iguanodon* to better understand its appearance and behavior.

Dino Fast Facts

Name meaning: "iguana tooth"
Type: Ornithischian
Period: early Cretaceous
Location: Belgium, England, Germany and Spain
Diet: herbivore

Mysterious Thumb Spikes

Iguanodon's hands had four fingers and a thumb spike, a sharp thumb-like appendage. In the 1800s, scientists thought the spike was located on the dinosaur's nose, like on an iguana. Even though we now know the spikes were on their hands, their purpose is still a mystery. One possibility is that they were weapons to defend against predators or to fight with other *Iguanodon*. Another possibility is that they were tools used when foraging for food, either to break open seeds and fruits or to strip leaves off of branches.

Iguanodon hand fossil

DO YOU KNOW ABOUT...

Ornithopods

Iguanodon was a type of Ornithischian called an ornithopod. Ornithopods usually had three toes on their back feet, and they were bipedal either some or all of the time. Since they were Ornithischians, they usually ate plants. Another ornithopod was *Heterodontosaurus*. Ornithopods were different from other subgroups of Ornithischians like armored dinosaurs (like *Stegosaurus* and *Ankylosaurus*) and ceratopsians (like *Triceratops*).

33 feet (10.1 meters)

The Real Iguanodon

Since *Iguanodon* was one of the first dinosaur specimens to be discovered, many early dinosaur fossils were incorrectly classified as *Iguanodon*. The name became so popular that similar dinosaurs on four different continents (Europe, Asia, Africa, and North America) were assigned it. Today, there are only two species of *Iguanodon*, called *Iguanodon bernissartensis* and *Iguanodon galvensis*. But a side effect of narrowing the classification was that the original specimen called *Iguanodon* is no longer considered part of the genus. It is now called *Therosaurus*.

DO YOU KNOW ABOUT...

Toothy Origins

The original discovery of *Iguanodon* was possibly an accident. Mary Ann Mantell, on a trip with her husband, supposedly noticed something odd peeking out of the ground. She picked it up and realized they were fossilized teeth remains. The teeth were analyzed by scientists, but they were unsure what creature the teeth belonged to. The closest match they could find was iguana teeth. This discovery would aid in the understanding and formation of the Dinosauria clade in 1842.

Mrs. MANTELL.
(From a painting in the possession of W. M. Woodhouse, Esq.)

Iguanodon's Walk

Iguanodon may have been able to walk on either two or four legs, depending on the situation. Based on tracks scientists have found, they likely walked on two legs most often. Walking on four legs would have been useful when looking for food near the ground, like ferns and horsetails, or when drinking water. Recent research suggests that *Iguanodon* walked with its back almost horizontal to the ground and its tail extended and raised to help it balance. *Iguanodon* had flat hooves on its fingers and toes.

Spinosaurus

Spinosaurus (spy-nuh-SAWR-us) is the largest known carnivorous dinosaur. Paleontologists estimate that it was 40 to 60 feet (12.2 to 18.3 meters) long and on average weighed 823 tons (746.6 metric tons). It is difficult to get a more exact number, because only partial *Spinosaurus* skeletons have been discovered. Much of what we think about *Spinosaurus* is still uncertain.

Dino Fast Facts

Name meaning: "spine lizard"
Type: Saurischian (theropod)
Period: mid Cretaceous
Location: Egypt and Morocco
Diet: carnivore

Spinosaurus' Sail

Spinosaurus was named for the spines on its back. The tallest spines were each about 5.4 feet (1.6 meters) long, and all the spines were connected by skin. Together, they are referred to as a sail. *Spinosaurus* most likely used its sail for display purposes, so it might have been brightly colored. It had flexible backbones, so it may have arched its back to make its sail appear larger. This would have made *Spinosaurus* look twice as big and more intimidating. The sail may also have been used to attract mates or to communicate. Other dinosaurs might have been able to tell from a sail how old that *Spinosaurus* was, how big it was, and what gender it was.

6 feet
(1.8 meters)

40-60 feet (12.2-18.3 meters)

The First Semiaquatic Dinosaur

Spinosaurus might have been the first dinosaur that could swim! It may have even spent most of its time in bodies of water like rivers and swamps but could also walk on land, making it semiaquatic. Its anatomy was adapted to this lifestyle. *Spinosaurus* had wide flat feet for walking in mud, high nostrils for breathing while partially underwater, and small back legs for paddling. Its skull was long and narrow like a crocodile skull. Its bones were heavy but compact like the bones of penguins. Its center of mass was far forward on its body, which made it easier to move in the water. This also made it harder to move on land, so when out of the water *Spinosaurus* probably needed to use all four of its feet.

DO YOU KNOW ABOUT...

Baby Spinosaurus

In 2018, researchers described a tiny bone as matching the shape of adult *Spinosaurus* toe bones, but much smaller. They think the bone belonged to a very young *Spinosaurus*. Since the bone has the same shape as the adult bones, which are adapted for swimming and walking on soft surfaces, *Spinosaurus* probably spent time in and near the water both as a juvenile and adult.

Seafood

Most of *Spinosaurus'* prey lived in water, specifically in rivers in North Africa. *Spinosaurus* was a piscivore, a carnivore that ate fish in particular. It probably even ate very large fish like sharks. *Spinosaurus* may have eaten like a pelican. It had an unusual jaw that could move flexibly and open very wide, so it would have been able to swallow smaller prey whole. Its teeth were different from the teeth of most theropods. They were shaped like cones instead of like curved blades. In 2004, a tooth from a dinosaur related to *Spinosaurus* was found in a pterosaur. So *Spinosaurus* and its relatives might not have been limited to aquatic animals as food.

Velociraptor

Velociraptor (vuh-LAH-suh-rap-ter) was a small and fast dinosaur. It was about 5 to 7 feet (1.5 to 2.1 meters) long and weighed about 30 pounds (13.6 kilograms). It could probably run up to 24 miles (38.6 kilometers) per hour. It has been portrayed in movies as much larger, because the *Velociraptor* in some films was modeled after a completely different dinosaur.

Dino Fast Facts

Name meaning: "swift plunderer"
Type: Saurischian (theropod)
Period: late Cretaceous
Location: Mongolia
Diet: carnivore

Feathered but Flightless

Velociraptor had quill knobs, the places where wing feathers are attached in birds. This proves that the dinosaur had feathered wings. *Velociraptor* might have had ancestors that could fly, but its front arms were too short for flying. It used its feathers for another purpose instead. Possibilities include attracting mates, protecting the nest, regulating body temperature, and running faster. Feathers were not *Velociraptor*'s only shared characteristic with modern birds. *Velociraptor* also had wishbones, laid eggs in nests, and had hollow bones.

←— 7 feet (2.1 meters) —→

6 feet (1.8 meters)

Hunting Behavior

Velociraptor was a small predator, and it had small prey. It probably ate little herbivorous dinosaurs, reptiles, insects, amphibians, and early mammals. Sometimes *Velociraptor* scavenged for food. There is also evidence of *Velociraptor* fighting larger dinosaurs like *Protoceratops*. It is possible that *Velociraptor* hunted in packs. All *Velociraptor* specimens have been found alone, but closely related dinosaurs have been discovered in groups. Either way, *Velociraptor* probably liked to sneak up on prey and surprise it. It probably had good night vision and was nocturnal.

DO YOU KNOW ABOUT...

Velociraptor's Intelligence

Velociraptor had a long skull and snout. Inside its mouth were up to 30 sharp teeth. Its brain was also large, considering the size of its body. It was probably smarter than many other dinosaurs. Carnivorous dinosaurs often had larger brains than herbivorous dinosaurs.

Death by Claws

Velociraptor had three curved claws on its hands. It also had a sharp, curved claw on the second toe of each of its back feet. The toe claws were about 3 inches (7.6 centimeters) long. *Velociraptor* usually held them off the ground, and it could retract them when it wasn't using them. When hunting, it could use the claws to keep hold of its prey. *Velociraptor* might also have stabbed prey in the stomach with its claws so the prey would bleed to death. This is the same method that saber-toothed tigers used much later.

Parasaurolophus

Parasaurolophus (pa-ruh-saw-RAH-luh-fus) was a hadrosaurid dinosaur, also called a duckbilled dinosaur. *Parasaurolophus* is one of the most popular hadrosaurids because of the interesting shape of its crest.

Dino Fast Facts

Name meaning: "like crested lizard"
Type: Ornithischian
Period: late Cretaceous
Location: United States and Canada
Diet: herbivore

Duckbilled Dinosaurs

Hadrosaurids were the dominant herbivore during the Cretaceous period. They were a type of ornithopod, like *Iguanodon*. They are called duckbilled dinosaurs because the front of their jawbones was flat and resembled those of ducks. However, the actual shape of their snout may have been very different from the bones. Also, hadrosaurids are not related to modern ducks, because ducks are descended from theropods. Paleontologists think hadrosaurids had a hinge between their upper jaw and the rest of their skull that allowed them to move their teeth up and down, side to side, and front to back. Hadrosaurids were also known for the crests on their heads. Different hadrosaurids had different types of crests, and *Parasaurolophus* had one of the largest and most uniquely shaped.

Parasaurolophus' Crest

Parasaurolophus' crest was a long tube made out of hollow bone attached to the top of its skull. It was probably used both for visual and auditory communication. Visually, the crest could have helped *Parasaurolophus* be recognizable to other dinosaurs, like the sail of *Spinosaurus*. Audibly, the empty space inside the crest connected to *Parasaurolophus*' throat and lungs so it worked like a resonating chamber. When the dinosaur made noises, they would be sent through the crest before leaving the mouth. This amplified the sound.

Juvenile Development

In 2009, a small *Parasaurolophus* specimen was found. It was about 8 feet (2.4 meters) long, one-fourth the size of an adult, and paleontologists named it Joe. Paleontologists can tell a dinosaur's age by the number of rings on its bones. Joe had no rings, so it must have died when it was less than one year old. Instead of a long curved crest, Joe had a small bump on its head. That means that *Parasaurolophus* started growing its crest when it was very young. Most dinosaurs with similar appendages do not start growing them until they are older, making *Parasaurolophus* unusual. The bump also means that juvenile *Parasaurolophus* would have had a higher voice than adults.

DO YOU KNOW ABOUT....

Other Hypotheses

In paleontology, like all areas of science, people make a hypothesis when trying to answer a question or solve a problem. Testing the hypothesis can support it or prove it wrong. Often it takes many incorrect hypotheses before the correct one is found. Here are some other, less popular hypotheses that researchers proposed for the use of *Parasaurolophus*' crest:

Hypothesis	Problems with hypothesis
To breathe underwater, like a snorkel	The crest did not have an opening on the end.
To hold air when the dinosaur was underwater	The crest was too small for storage.
To support the dinosaur's head and neck	The crest was not attached to the neck.
To improve the dinosaur's sense of smell	*Parasaurolophus* probably didn't need a strong sense of smell.
To hold salt, like the glands found in marine animals	*Parasaurolophus* may not have lived by the ocean.
To hold plants out of the way	*Parasaurolophus* ate plants and was unlikely to avoid them.
To attach to a proboscis, like an elephant's truck	Prabosces usually attach at the front of the head.
To fight or defend against other animals	Weapons usually point away from the body.

Ankylosaurus

Ankylosaurus (ang-kuh-lo-SAWR-us) was one of the largest armored dinosaurs. The biggest specimen found so far was over 20 feet (6.1 meters) long and probably weighed more than 4 tons (3.6 metric tons). Because of its size and sturdiness, people often compare *Ankylosaurus* to a military tank!

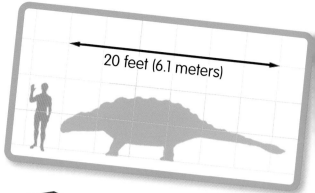

20 feet (6.1 meters)

Dino Fast Facts

Name meaning: "fused lizard"
Type: Ornithischian
Period: late Cretaceous
Location: United States and Canada
Diet: herbivore

Defensive Armor

Ankylosaurus had many plates made out of bone attached to its skin. They are called osteoderms, meaning "bone skin," and they are the same structure found on crocodiles and armadillos. *Ankylosaurus'* osteoderms covered its back, sides, tail, and head. They were especially concentrated around its neck. The osteoderms were too hard for any predator to bite through, so *Ankylosaurus'* only area of weakness was its stomach. In addition to the plates, *Ankylosaurus* had rows of spikes on its sides and horns on its head. Its armor was probably very heavy. *Ankylosaurus* had short, wide limbs that kept it low to the ground and supported its body. It walked very slowly, only a little faster than a turtle.

Tail Club

Ankylosaurus had a powerful weapon at the end of its tail. The last vertebrae in its tail interlocked with each other and were surrounded by more osteoderms. This created a thick bony club that the dinosaur could swing at attackers. A large *Ankylosaurus* with a large tail could have broken another dinosaur's bones! *Ankylosaurus* may have used its tail for other reasons, like attracting mates. But two specimens have been found with damaged tail clubs, so it may have sometimes been used as a weapon.

DO YOU KNOW ABOUT...

Ankylosaurus Didn't Fit In

Ankylosaurus belonged to a group of dinosaurs called ankylosaurs. They all had osteoderms. But compared to the other ankylosaurs, *Ankylosaurus* looked unusual. For example, its teeth were much smaller, and its body was much bigger. Its nostrils were on the side of its snout instead of in the front like on other ankylosaurs. Also, all ankylosaurs' armor did not look the same. One ankylosaur had osteoderms on its hips, and another had spikes on its shoulders. *Ankylosaurus* may have lacked these features.

Gargoyleosaurus

Ankylosaurus' Diet

Ankylosaurus was a herbivore that probably ate whatever low-growing plants were available. It had a good sense of smell for finding food and a small beak for stripping leaves off plants. Its skull was wide, short, and triangular. Its teeth were not strong enough to chew the plants it ate, but its rib cage was very wide. This means it probably fermented its food in its stomach. Ankylosaurs in general had a large hyoid bone, a bone that supports the tongue. Therefore, *Ankylosaurus* may have had a large and flexible tongue.

Triceratops

Triceratops (try-SER-uh-tahps) was a herbivorous dinosaur that lived up to the end of the Cretaceous period and the mass extinction that accompanied it. Its skin may have been covered in bristles.

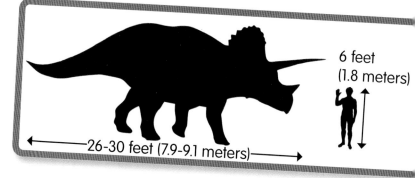

6 feet (1.8 meters)

←—26-30 feet (7.9-9.1 meters)—→

Dino Fast Facts

Name meaning: "three-horned face"
Type: Ornithischian
Period: late Cretaceous
Location: United States
Diet: herbivore

Bigheaded

Triceratops' head was so big that sometimes it was a third of the dinosaur's length. The largest *Triceratops* skull found so far is about 8 feet (2.4 meters) long. *Triceratops* had a large skull with a frill and three horns. Two of the horns were on its forehead and one was on its snout. The horns were probably used to defend against predators and to fight with other *Triceratops*. They have been found damaged, including one showing healed bite marks that match *Tyrannosaurus'* teeth. *Triceratops'* frill could grow to 6 feet (1.8 meters) across. It may have strengthened *Triceratops'* jaw. It also might have been used to control the dinosaur's body temperature. Or it might have been for display, either to attract potential mates or to warn away potential predators.

Toothy

Triceratops had more complicated teeth than any other dinosaur. Its teeth were also more complicated than those of any modern reptile or mammal. They were made up of five different types of tissue. For comparison, horses have four tissue types and most reptiles have two. This sophistication meant that *Triceratops* could use its teeth in different ways, from splitting food into two pieces to crushing it. *Triceratops*' adaptability made it a more effective grazer. It could eat food from a variety of plants, including ferns, cycads, and small palm trees. Paleontologists think this is why *Triceratops* was a dominant herbivore during the late Cretaceous period.

DO YOU KNOW ABOUT...

How Many Teeth?

Like *Diplodocus*, *Triceratops* replaced the teeth it lost. It had up to 800 teeth in its mouth, and it used a few hundred of them at a time. The teeth were in groups called batteries. A battery had 36 to 40 columns of teeth on each side of *Triceratops*' jaw. A column in a battery had three to five teeth. When the set of teeth being used became worn, it was replaced by teeth from the closest battery.

Torosaurus

Who Was Torosaurus?

Some paleontologists think *Triceratops* and *Torosaurus*, another Cretaceous dinosaur, were the same animal. Both dinosaurs had frills, but *Torosaurus*' frill was larger and had two holes in it. *Triceratops*' frill expanded throughout the dinosaur's life, so researchers thought it might be a younger version of *Torosaurus*. Specifically, they proposed that *Torosaurus* remains are the remains of *Triceratops* who lived an unusually long time. However, some *Torosaurus* bones may not be fully mature. If the dinosaurs were the same species, there should be no young *Torosaurus* specimens. The debate is still continuing.

Tyrannosaurus

Like *Triceratops*, *Tyrannosaurus* (tuh-ra-nuh-SAWR-us) was one of the last dinosaurs to live before dinosaurs went extinct. In fact, *Tyrannosaurus* was the main predator of *Triceratops*. *Tyrannosaurus* was a large, powerful carnivore that could bite through bone. It is probably the most well-known dinosaur. *Tyrannosaurus* contained one species, *Tyrannosaurus rex*, which is often abbreviated as *T. rex*.

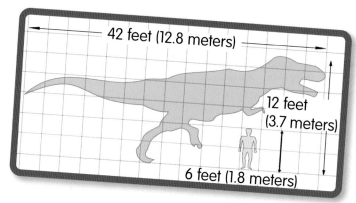

42 feet (12.8 meters)

12 feet (3.7 meters)

6 feet (1.8 meters)

Dino Fast Facts

Name meaning: "tyrant lizard"
Type: Saurischian (theropod)
Period: late Cretaceous
Location: United States and Canada
Diet: carnivore

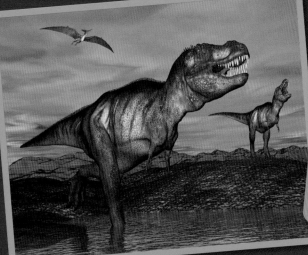

How Did Tyrannosaurus Walk?

Tyrannosaurus had a very large, heavy head. To balance its weight, it walked with its body held horizontally and its tail raised behind it. *Tyrannosaurus* had strong thighs to support it and help it walk long distances. It was not as fast as smaller theropods, though. It was probably able to move 10 to 25 miles (16.1 to 40.2 kilometers) per hour. In contrast to *Tyrannosaurus*' legs, its arms were extremely small. This may have been because its neck muscles took up more space. *Tyrannosaurus* needed a very strong neck to support its large head. It did not need long arms, and in fact they might have been more trouble to take care of.

DO YOU KNOW ABOUT...

Useless Arms?

Paleontologists still do not know the purpose of *Tyrannosaurus*' very short arms. One theory is that they were used to hold onto prey. Other researchers think that they may have been entirely useless! They are trying to reconstruct the muscles of *Tyrannosaurus*' arms to learn more about how they might have been used.

How Did Tyrannosaurus Eat?

The teeth of most theropods were flat and pointed like knives. *Tyrannosaurus'* teeth, on the other hand, were wider, rounder, and less sharp. They were like having a mouth full of spikes. This shape made it harder for prey to escape *Tyrannosaurus'* grasp. The largest carnivore tooth to be discovered is a *Tyrannosaurus* tooth. It is 12 inches (30.5 centimeters) long. When *Tyrannosaurus* used its teeth to bite, the result was about ten times stronger than the bite of a shark.

DO YOU KNOW ABOUT...

Predator or Scavenger?

Some paleontologists think *Tyrannosaurus* was not a predator at all. Its small eyes and arms would have made it harder to see and hold onto prey. Its large legs would have made it slower but better at walking long distances scavenging for food. However, a recent finding showed that a duckbilled dinosaur was bitten by a *T. rex* and later healed, meaning it was attacked while it was alive. Many paleontologists think *Tyrannosaurus* both hunted and scavenged, depending on the availability of food.

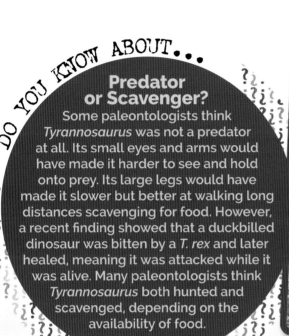

Yutyrannus

Tyrannosaurus Might Have Had Feathers

Some dinosaurs that were closely related to *Tyrannosaurus* had feathers. One was *Dilong*. It was smaller than *Tyrannosaurus* and covered in shaggy feathers. Another was *Yutyrannus*, which was much larger than *Dilong* but also feathered. These dinosaurs' feathers mean that *Tyrannosaurus* might have had them too. Additionally, *Tyrannosaurus* lived at the end of the Mesozoic era, and later carnivorous dinosaurs were more likely to have feathers. For now, whether *Tyrannosaurus* was scaly or soft remains a mystery.

Dilong

Glossary

Amplify – to increase

Appendage – a small body part that sticks out from the rest of the body

Aquatic – living mainly or entirely in water

Archosaur – a type of reptile like a dinosaur, pterosaur, or crocodile

Auxiliary – extra or supplemental

Basal – having to do with the foundation or beginning

Biped – an animal that walks on two feet

Carnivore – an animal that eats animals

Clade – a group of taxa with all the descendants of one ancestor; an unranked taxon

Continent – a division of land on Earth, like Africa or Europe

Digitigrade – walking on the digits (toes or fingers) with the heel off the ground

Domain – the highest-ranking taxon for classifying animals

Dominant – more powerful than the rest

Dwarfism – when an animal is significantly smaller than the average size for its species

Era – a span of 1 billion years

Evolve – to change over time through gradual changes

Extinct – not existing anymore

Facultative – happening in some situations and not in others

Ferment – to break down or change chemically

Forage – to search for food

Fossil – something preserved from a past geologic time

Furcula – a forked bone found in modern birds, also called a wishbone

Gastrolith – a stone swallowed by an animal used to crush plant matter in its digestive system

Genus – the taxon ranked above species and below family

Geologic era – a division of geologic time smaller than an eon and larger than a period

Geologic period – a division of geologic time smaller than an era and larger than an epoch

Geology – the science of the history of earth and the life on it

Herbivore – an animal that eats plants

High browser – an animal that eats plants found in high places

Juvenile – a young animal

Low browser – an animal that eats plants found in low places

Nocturnal – active at night

Omnivore – an animal that eats both plants and animals

Opposable – able to face and be placed against another digit

Order – the taxon ranked above family and below class

Paleontologist – a scientist who uses fossils to study plants and animals from past geologic periods

Period – a unit of time that describes various parts of an era

Piscivore – an animal that eats fish

Plantigrade – walking on the sole of the foot with the heel touching the ground

Predator – an animal that preys on other animals for food

Prey – an animal that is caught by another animal and eaten

Proboscis – a long trunk or snout

Quadruped – an animal that walks on four feet

Reptile – an animal that breathes air, has scales or plates, and moves on short legs or its stomach

Resonating chamber – a space that uses vibration to increase the intensity of a sound

Scavenger – an animal that eats other animals that are already dead

Semiaquatic – living in water sometimes or most of the time, and on land sometimes

Serrated – having notched edges, similar to a saw

Skeleton – the bones of an animal, which support it and protect its organs

Species – a group of animals that are genetically similar and can reproduce

Specimen – an individual example of a group

Supercontinent – a large land mass consisting of multiple continents, like Pangaea millions of years ago

Terrestrial – living mainly or entirely on land

Therapsid – a small mammal ancestor that shared many traits with modern-day mammals

Thermoregulation – the process of controlling body temperature

Tissue – a material animals are made out of

Vertebra – one of the bones in the backbone

Index